AF885472

Auto Accidents, Personal Injuries, And Wrongful Death Lawsuits

Information That May Be Helpful If You or A Loved One Have Been Injured Or Killed Due To The Negligence or Wrongdoing of Others

W. Bradley Parker, Esq.

ISBN: 978-1-941645-42-0

Designed and Published by:
Speakeasy Publications
73-03 Bell Blvd #10
Oakland Gardens, N.Y. 11364
www.SpeakeasyMarketingInc.com
(888) 225-8594

DISCLAIMER

This publication is intended to be informational only. No legal advice is being given and no attorney-client relationship is intended to be created by reading this material. If you are facing legal issues, whether criminal or civil, seek professional legal counsel to get your questions answered.

PARKER LAW FIRM

TRIAL LAWYERS

Parker Law Firm
2317 Plaza Parkway, Suite 100
Bedford, TX 76021
(817) 503-9200
www.parkerlawfirm.com
brad@parkerlawfirm.com

Client Testimonials

"I will always give a strong recommendation about the Parker Law Firm, because they are aggressive defenders of the Truth and that is what I needed to guarantee a successful outcome."

- *Terence R.*

....

"After being injured in an automobile accident, I was unsure of what to do and felt overwhelmed. The attorneys and staff at the Parker Law Firm helped and obtained a successful outcome for me. I was pleased with the quality and professionalism I always felt when contacting their office. I highly recommend the Parker Law Firm if you have been injured."

- *Carolyn M.*

....

"I was a passenger injured in an accident, when the insurance company would no longer respond to phone calls, emails, or my request of reimbursement for medical bills and compensation of time lost from work; I was referred to Parker Law Firm by a lifelong friend. I am extremely happy I decided to go in this direction; it was a weight off my shoulders to have someone else take care of dealing with the insurance company. Dealing with The Parker Law Firm was so easy as they kept me informed and before I knew it I had a settlement. Do not hesitate to contact this Law Firm you will not regret it!!!"

- *Kelley B.*

"When I walked in the office the first day, we felt welcome. The whole team is very professional. Mr. Parker led me in the right direction and got everything done to our satisfaction, also in a timely manner. We selected Parker Law Firm for their professionalism and they never made me feel like I had no idea I knew what I was doing. I never had to send items twice. He came across as honest and trustworthy which, in the end, he proved. Lead us in the right direction, always returned our calls, let us know what to expect with each and every person we had to talk with, calmed me during my deposition and gave us hope. His secretary was a great help with everything we needed to supply her. Very well organized and never lost anything. Mr. Parker is a real professional and knows his laws well. Never had to look up laws, never said he would get back with us. Mr. Parker always left each session with all questions answered. Mr. Parker is the best I've met and would suggest no other. His law firm gets what they promise. I'm doing very well thanks to Parker Law Firm."

- Joel & Pam C.

....

"Thank you again for all you did. You'll never be forgotten. In fact I'd recommend you, yelling from the rooftops! May God always bless you in whatever your hands find to do! Love you lots and appreciate you!"

- Alice W.

Table Of Contents

AUTHOR INTRODUCTION

Attorney W. Bradley Parker obtained his bachelor's degree from the University of Texas at Austin in 1982 and his law degree from Texas Tech University School of Law in 1985. After law school, Mr. Parker was a trial lawyer with a large Fort Worth firm. He then formed the firm of Watson & Parker and then Noteboom & Parker, before establishing Parker Law Firm.

Mr. Parker's practice has focused exclusively in the area of trial work since he was licensed in 1985. He has an unwavering commitment to people who have been seriously harmed or killed by the negligence or wrongdoing of others. His practice focuses on those who have been killed or seriously injured in major trucking and motor vehicle crashes, by dangerous drugs and medical devices, in aviation accidents and industrial catastrophes, or whose lives have been seriously disrupted or even destroyed by the bad faith conduct of an insurance company.

Built on years of trial experience, a tradition of personal service and a well-deserved reputation for zealous representation of his clients, Mr. Parker and his firm are dedicated to the timely delivery of outstanding results.

Mr. Parker has been Board Certified by the Texas Board of Specialization in Personal Injury Trial Law since 1997. Less than 2% of the lawyers licensed to practice law in Texas are Board Certified in Personal Injury Trial Law.

Mr. Parker has been repeatedly recognized and honored by his peers to lead in various legal organizations in which he is a member. He most recently served as the 2013 President of the Texas Trial Lawyers Association. He is past President of the Tarrant County Trial Lawyers Association, the Tarrant County Bar Association, and past Chairman of the Texas Trial Lawyers Association Advocates. He is also a sustaining member of the American Association of Justice, Director of the Texas Trial Lawyers Association, member of the Dallas and Tarrant County Trial Lawyers Association, Tarrant County Bar Association and Tarrant County Bar Foundation. Mr. Parker is also a member of the American Board of Trial Advocates.

Mr. Parker has an "A.V." rating, the highest rating awarded by Martindale-Hubbell lawyer rating directory. From 2002 through the present, Mr. Parker has been repeatedly recognized by ***Fort Worth, Texas Magazine*** as one of Fort Worth's "Attorneys worth knowing" and a Texas Super Lawyer (2003, 2006-present) by Thomson Reuters as published in Texas Monthly Magazine.

Education, Memberships and Recognitions

- B.A. University of Texas at Austin, 1982
- J.D. Texas Tech University School of Law, 1985
- Member, State Bar of Texas, 1985 - present
- Board Certified, Personal Injury Trial Law, Texas Board of Legal Specialization, 1997 - present
- Member, College of the State Bar of Texas, current
- President, Tarrant County Trial Lawyers Association, 1998 - 1999
- Texas Trial Lawyers Association
    - Chair, Texas Trial Lawyers Association Advocates, 1999
    - Member, Board of Directors, 1998 - present
    - Vice President - Legislative Affairs, 2011
    - President, 2013
- Tarrant County Bar Association
    - Member, Board of Directors, 2004 - 2011
    - President, 2010 - 2011
- Life Fellow, Texas Bar Foundation, 2009 - present
- Life Fellow, Tarrant County Bar Foundation, 2006 - present
- Member, District 7A Grievance Committee, State Bar of Texas, 2004 - 2008
- Panel Chair, District 7A Grievance Committee, State Bar of Texas, 2006 - 2008
- Member, American Board of Trial Advocates (ABOTA), 2006 - present
- Fort Worth Magazine, Top Attorneys, 2002 - present
- Texas Monthly, Super Lawyer, (2003, 2006 – present) by Thompson Reuters as published in Texas Monthly Magazine.
- Master, Mahon Inn of Court, 2011 – 2016
- Emeritus, Mahon Inn of Court 2016 - present

Factors That Constitute A Viable Personal Injury Claim

There are at least three different things that factor into a viable personal injury claim. The first and foremost factor is how significant are the injuries. A minor injury of course is not going to make for a very large claim. The more significant the injury the more significant the claim. That is not to say that a minor injury cannot support a viable claim. It only means that the more serious the injury the more significant the claim.

The next factor is liability. Who is responsible for causing the event? Was it solely the fault of the other party or do both parties share blame? Were there other factors that were responsible, at least in part, for causing the event? How culpable are each of the parties and what were the underlying motivating factors? These are but a few of the questions surrounding the liability issue and the answer to these questions will play a vital role in the value of the claim.

The last factor is probably the most misunderstood – causation. Did the event cause the injury? This may seem simple but it is anything but simple. Imagine a car crash in which your back suffers multiple herniated discs. But what if your back had been

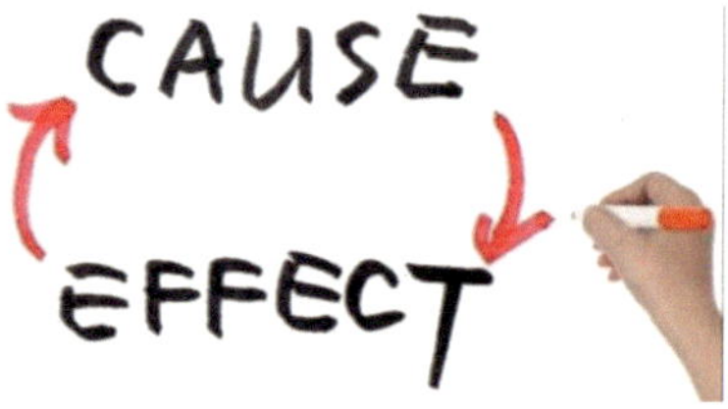

operated on before. Or that while you had not had an actual surgery you had been seeing a chiropractor or orthopedic surgeon for months due to pain. The question will arise as to whether your back was injured as a result of the crash or due to a pre-existing injury. You can certainly guess what position the insurance company is going to take.

The short answer is that all of these factors must be present in order to have a viable claim. Notwithstanding the presence of each of the three factors, the insurance company will attack each factor in an effort to minimize or even eliminate the claim.

Even if you were hit by drunken driver of an eighteen wheeler truck and your car is completely totaled, if you walk away with nothing more than a scratch, then that is not a significant claim from the standpoint of the value of the claim. Whereas, if you were hit by a nun returning from church resulting in a small dent to the back of your car, but it knocks your head into the car pillar in such a way that results in a brain injury -- that makes for a very different type of claim. The bottom line is that you cannot always factor in what you think is obvious -- the drunken eighteen wheeler trucker versus the nun. All three factors have to be fully evaluated in determining the viability of a claim.

Importance Of Seeking Medical Attention Right After An Accident

At the Parker Law Firm, we rarely handle any case where medical treatment has not been obtained almost immediately. If the injuries are serious then immediate medical attention is almost always obtained. There are certainly times when the

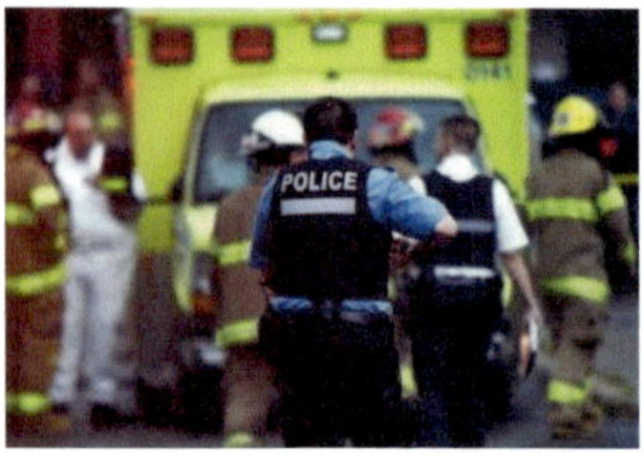

significance of the injury is not readily apparent and there may be some delay in obtaining medical treatment. But if you are hurt, you need to go to the doctor as soon as humanly possible. By delaying you are just providing a defense to the insurance company that will minimize your claim. They will take the position that you must not be very hurt if you did not seek medical treatment; delayed in seeking medical treatment; or did not follow up on that treatment as directed by the health care provider.

However, the opposite of that is sometimes true as well. There can be initial treatment for what is believed to be a minor back injury and then no treatment for a period of time in the hope that the pain will resolve. After all, back injuries often heal on their own, it just takes time. But if over time the injury either does not get better or even gets worse before further treatment is sought the picture can become clouded as to whether there has been a subsequent injury.

The bottom line is that if you are hurt, you need to get to the doctor and you need to follow up with your doctor's appointments and do exactly what they say. You should see a doctor as soon as possible. The fact that you do not seek immediate medical treatment is not necessarily devastating to a case but it will raise issues as to why the delay and how serious the injury really is.

Importance Of Following A Doctor's Advice

It is extremely important to follow your doctor's advice on treatment and rehabilitation. If the doctor says, "Go to physical therapy", you need to go to physical therapy. The reason is very simple. First and foremost, you need to get well. But secondly, the insurance companies will look at that and make a determination that, "If you didn't go to physical therapy like your doctor said you should, then you must not be that hurt; or if you are hurt, it's because you didn't follow the doctor's advice". While we know that may not necessarily be the case that is a very powerful argument in front of a jury.

You have always got to keep in mind what are the twelve people on the jury going to think about your behavior, and especially your behavior in getting well and getting treated by the doctor. If they believe that, "Part of the reason you are hurt is because you didn't do what the doctor said", they are not likely to compensate you as much as you might otherwise deserve. Insurance companies know this, they understand this, and they play on this. If they see that you are not following your doctor's advice or you are not getting treatment, they know they can use that to minimize the value of your claim.

Importance Of Evidence And Witnesses In A Personal Injury Claim

Evidence is extremely important. Oftentimes, there are questions about who did what and when. So many times, especially in the more horrific and serious injury cases, the person who has been injured may not remember, or heaven forbid, may have been killed as a result of the injuries. This results in numerous questions as to exactly what happened. It may be that the only person who can tell us what happened is the person you are suing. So, it is vitally important, and especially in the more serious injury cases, that an attorney board certified in personal injury trial law be hired sooner rather than later. The sooner you hire a board certified attorney the sooner that evidence can be gathered.

The types of evidence that may need to be obtained quickly often includes scene evidence such as skid marks; gouge marks on the pavement; testing of materials; inspections of the vehicles involved; retrieval of phone records; the retention of experts and taking of witness statements. Witnesses move and often time feel less compelled to assist with the passage of time. Thus there is importance of speaking to them as soon as possible. The more significant the event, the more likely that the insurance companies will be on the scene almost immediately. Therefore, it is very important to secure

both the evidence and get witness statements as soon as possible before anything changes or the evidence is destroyed either on purpose or by accident. Having a car repaired before it can be inspected can destroy evidence and eliminate clues as to what happened. Cell phone data is often only preserved for a certain period of time and a delay in seeking information may make it impossible to obtain. Securing evidence and preserving it as soon as possible is often times extremely important.

Is Your Personal Injury Claim Doomed If There Are No Witnesses Or Evidence?

Not necessarily. There are occasions when theories can be developed in other ways. However, when there is no evidence or witnesses it can make the claim much more susceptible to being minimized or even defeated. Each case presents its own unique set of circumstances and it is on a case by case basis as to what the effect of not having evidence or late developed evidence will have overall. The bottom line is that it is much easier to gather evidence when it is fresh than after several months. By hiring a competent and board certified personal injury lawyer early in the process, the gathering of evidence in the claim can be maximized.

Keeping A Journal Of Events After An Accident

We recommend to all of our clients that they keep some type of journal documenting what they go through with the treatment of and recovery from their injuries. Any journal prepared by our client for communicating with us can usually be protected by the attorney / client privilege. The reason we want our clients to keep a journal is because oftentimes, the recovery process can take weeks, months, or even years. During that period of time, people typically do not remember specifically how they felt or what they were going through three, six, twelve or twenty-four months ago. It is very important that we have those notes to look back at to have a clear understanding of what our client has been through in the treatment and recovery process, the pain, the mental anguish that they suffered, the impairment that they endured. All of this is compensable, meaning it can be compensated. By having a journal we are able to then communicate clearly and accurately to the defense or even the jury what all our client has been through.

We also want to know about our client's appointments, visits and how they felt at that time so that we can compare it with what the medical records say. We want to be sure to know about every doctor that they have seen and every appointment that they have been to.

Dealing With Insurance Companies

Never under any circumstance should you give a statement or talk to the other side's insurance company, and frankly, probably not even your own, unless and until you hire an attorney. The insurance companies will typically contact the victims of an accident almost immediately wanting to get a statement from them. They do it in a very innocuous and innocent type of way to make the person think, "Oh, they're just gathering information." But what they are really gathering are facts to help minimize or even defeat your claim. They are also trying to get some idea of the scope and extent of your injury. The problem is that you may not even be aware of the exact extent or nature of your injury and therefore, they may commit you to a description of an injury that is not accurate.

Again, they are trying to minimize or undermine your claim. You will ultimately have to give a statement if the case goes into litigation, because they will probably want to take your deposition. Even in the cases that do not go into litigation, we often times will work with the insurance companies to provide our client's statement in an effort to cooperate and move the case forward, but only after we have a full understanding of the extent of the injuries, the duration of the same, the extent of treatment necessary as well as exactly what happened on the day of the accident. Failure to have a full understanding can lead to significant issues later down the line.

MISCONCEPTIONS ABOUT PERSONAL INJURY CLAIMS IN TEXAS

The number one thing that people are surprised at is how complicated these cases can be. Many people believe that if you get hurt, there is insurance out there and the insurance company is going to take care of you. That is a big misconception. Insurance companies are in business to make money for their shareholders and businesses do not make money by paying claims. If an insurance company can minimize or even avoid paying a claim they are in essence making money. Not only do the insurance companies search for ways to avoid paying a claim, there

are third parties that want a part of any recovery obtained. Doctors, hospitals and health insurance companies are but some of the third parties that may have liens, subrogation interests and contractual rights to a portion or all of any recovery obtained from an insurance company.

All too often people will decide to try and go it alone in filing their claims only to discover several months later that they are no closer to resolving the matter than when they started. The delay in hiring a lawyer will often times cause issues in recovering evidence, locating witnesses, and in processing the claim itself. Personal Injury claims are much more complicated than most people think and therefore hiring a competent, board certified lawyer sooner rather than later is usually always advisable.

"Personal Injury Lawyers Are Sleazy"

Often times people will delay hiring a lawyer because of the misconception about personal injury lawyers in general – that they are slimy, disingenuous, or untrustworthy. Unfortunately, these misconceptions are often fostered by TV advertisers with people screaming their alleged qualifications and to hire them, or by cheesy ambulance chasing stereotypes that are seen on some billboards.

Of course those types of lawyers do exist, but that is not what we are about at Parker Law Firm. You will not see us screaming on TV. You will not even see us on TV. Our clients overwhelmingly come to us through referrals from former clients and other attorneys. A referral from a former client or another attorney is considered as one of the highest compliments that we can receive.

Referrals are based on trust and respect and we absolutely honor that. When we meet with potential clients they are immediately impressed by the level of professionalism and caring that our firm exhibits. At Parker Law Firm, our clients are not just another number. Rather they are a real person with a real and unique problem. At Parker Law Firm, People Matter and we strive to make each and every client feel as though they are a part of our family. We strive to make certain that they stay fully informed every step of the process. We like to believe that after the very first visit, we have begun to change their perception of personal injury attorneys and specifically those at Parker Law Firm.

Is Filing A Personal Injury Claim An Easy Process?

Making a claim is easy. Getting the insurance company to honor the claim and fairly pay it is very difficult. As a general rule, the insurance companies fight tooth and nail to minimize if not outright avoid paying a claim. They typically contest the extent of injury as well as necessity for substantial portions of medical treatment. The insurance company will blame the injured party for their own injuries and rely on legal technicalities to diminish the claim as much as possible.

In addition, once the money is paid the next problem is keeping the money. There are doctor bills, hospital bills, health insurance companies – all of which have potentially significant legal rights to all or a portion of the proceeds through liens, subrogation or contractual rights. These entities must be negotiated with to allow a recovery. Often times it is more difficult fighting off these interests than it is fighting to get the compensation in the first place.

The legal hurdles involving these issues are significant and some statutes make it a crime not to honor the subrogation interests of governmental programs. In short, it is easy to file a claim. Getting fairly compensated and being able to keep the recovery is very complicated.

Do Most Personal Injury Cases Go To Trial Or Reach Settlement?

Most cases do reach a settlement and the ones that go to trial typically do so because of one of two reasons. The parties just cannot see eye to eye on the value of the case, or the insurance company knows that the lawyer is not very skilled at trial or does not have their case ready to go to trial. At Parker Law Firm we work every case up from day one as if it is going to trial. We do not consider there to be any other alternative than trial. As a result of preparing the case for trial combined with the fact of having more than thirty years of trial experience, typically the insurance company will settle with us for top value prior to going to trial.

Insurance companies will often settle claims for another reason too. They will often settle the case because the attorney is not as competent or skilled as they should be and the insurance company knows they can settle the claim on the cheap. Pennies on the dollar so to speak.

So you have two factors working in most settlements. They will settle the claim on the cheap if they think they can with an inexperienced or unprepared attorney, or they will ultimately settle for fair value because they know they run the risk of having to go to trial against a competent well prepared lawyer that is not afraid to go to court.

In order to obtain the very best result it is imperative that the case be worked up thoroughly and properly and by an aggressive, competent and skilled board certified personal injury attorney.

Timeframe For Resolution Of A Personal Injury Claim In Texas

There is no uniform amount of time in which a claim gets resolved. One of the biggest factors is "How long does it take for you to recover from your injuries?" If you can recover within three months, then the process of getting the claim resolved will be shorter than if it takes a year to recover from your injuries. The reason for this is simple. When you resolve your personal injury case – whether because of settlement or trial -- it is a onetime thing. You can never go back. If you were to settle your injury claim before you are fully healed, then what happens if you have a flare-up, or if complications arise? You cannot go back and get more money for the claim because you have already resolved the matter.

On average claims are resolved anywhere from 6 – 24 months from the date of hiring a lawyer, depending upon how quickly medical treatment is completed. Each case and each injury is different and there is no one size fits all.

Mistakes That Are Detrimental To Favorable Resolution Of A Personal Injury Claim

Failing to go to the doctor or do what the doctor prescribes is the number one thing that dooms any claim.

Number two, social media. So often, people will say something on social media that can be taken out of context to make them seem uninjured. The insurance companies will say things like, "Well, you must not be too hurt because you were doing this on social media". Too many people like to "check in" where they are going or send pictures of their vacation or those kinds of things. The defendants and insurance companies search the web and social media just as we do and can often times find things that when taken out of context tend to minimize the claim. We know that is not the truth. You do not have to live your life at home locked inside your closet just because you are hurt; you can still get out and do things, but they use those things to minimize and devalue your case. There is no end to what an insurance company will do to avoid liability or minimize it.

We always advise our clients to be very careful about what they are posting on social media. They can live their lives, but they do not need to broadcast it to the entire world.

Should Fee Be A Factor When Hiring A Personal Injury Attorney?

All personal injury attorneys work on a contingency fee basis, meaning they do not get paid unless and until you get paid. And so money should not be a roadblock to hiring a competent attorney to represent you. What you do need to be careful about though, are attorneys who will work on the cheap. Typically, the fee in a personal injury matter will be anywhere from 33 1/3% - 40% depending upon the type and the complexity of the case.

If an attorney says he is going to do it for twenty percent or something in that nature, be aware. There is a strong chance that either they do not know what they are doing or they are not very competent at what they are doing. Always remember the old adage that "you get what you pay for." It is better to pay the average or a little more to get a qualified board-certified personal injury trial lawyer who has a proven track record than to be a number or a cog in a wheel of some mass accident firm that has hundreds and hundreds of clients and you are nothing but a number. You are not going to get very good representation and you will not get the best value for your claim.

People often also think that after paying their attorney and the medical bills that there will be nothing left for them. While this might be true with some firms, at Parker Law Firm, our fee will NEVER be more than your recovery!!!!

We have an unwavering commitment to people who have been seriously harmed by the negligence or wrongdoing of others. Our practice focuses on those who have been killed or seriously injured in major trucking and motor vehicle accidents, by dangerous drugs and medical devices, suffered on the job injuries, in industrial catastrophes, or whose lives have been seriously disrupted or even destroyed by the bad faith conduct of an insurance company. We routinely handle brain injuries, burn victims, product liability matters, premises liability cases, dog bite cases, drowning accidents, amputation injuries as well all other serious injury or death matters.

We take great pride in the fact that each of our clients is treated as a person and not a number. When a client hires Parker Law Firm they are provided personal and individualized attention as if they were our only client and a member of our family. It is our mission and commitment to not only resolve each case on the best possible terms but to do so in a fashion and manner that keeps our clients fully informed and involved in each step of the process.

Additionally, our fee will NEVER exceed your recovery!

Motivation For Practicing Personal Injury Law

Helping people and holding those who have harmed others accountable is what drives us at the Parker Law Firm and was the fundamental reason why Brad Parker became an attorney. When someone has suffered a serious injury or the loss of a loved one, they are often times very vulnerable or just need help in dealing with the overwhelming issues that arise and come at them from every direction. The injured and their families become subjected to a process and system that they did not expect, do not understand and cannot easily navigate. At the Parker Law Firm we pride ourselves on being able to help our clients in not only being fairly compensated for their injuries, but in navigating the issues of subrogation, liens, medical expenses and bill collectors. It is important to us that you feel you are part of our family and you will always be treated as such.

Brad Parker has always been for the underdog. He was inspired to become a lawyer in many respects by observing the injustices people often times had to endure at the hands of insurance companies and corporations. Having been raised by a hard working blue collar father, he was instilled with a fundamental sense of right and wrong. He saw at an early age the abuses that insurance companies often inflict on people – simply for filing a claim.

The callous disregard of people by insurance companies and corporations is inherently wrong and should never be tolerated. As such, Brad determined that by becoming a lawyer that he could hold wrongdoers accountable for their actions and seeing that those who have suffered serious injuries and loss could be fairly compensated to the highest extent possible. Having worked first hand at the beginning of his career for a corporate law firm Brad quickly realized that it is much more satisfying to be able to help honest, hardworking, everyday people as opposed to insurance companies and corporate America.

Unique Attributes Of Attorney Brad Parker And Parker Law Firm In Handling Personal Injury Cases

You are not a number when you walk into the Parker Law Firm. You are a human being with a real problem that has real issues and real consequences. We understand that this process is not natural for you and that you may feel somewhat overwhelmed. We understand and appreciate that upfront.

From the day you walk into our law firm you will have a sense of relief, knowing that you have walked into the right place. When you hire us we take over every aspect relating to your personal injury claim so that you can concentrate on getting back on your feet as soon as possible.

When you hire us, we take over dealing with your medical providers, the medical billing companies and the insurance companies. We are there to help you every step of the way. You need to be concentrating on getting better, getting your life put back in shape and getting back in order. We take on the problems associated with seeking and getting medical treatment – from billing issues to subrogation and lien matters and everything else in between. We are there not only as your lawyer but as a friend and confidant. Our clients are family to us and we try in every way imaginable to alleviate those issues from your life so that you can concentrate on what is most important -- your health.

The majority of our clients come as referrals from past clients and other attorneys. That speaks legends about the quality of services provided to our clients by Parker Law Firm.

Medical Bills, Liens, And Subrogation Interests

One of the things that we always do on all of our personal injury cases and one of the many things that sets us apart from other law firms is that we negotiate your medical bills, negotiate the liens and negotiate the subrogation interests.

Many times, insurance will not cover a particular procedure or treatment or there are deductibles or co-pays that add up. We negotiate with the medical professionals and routinely receive a better rate, a better discount for your medical bills and a better reduction of the lien and subrogation amounts. All too often medical providers attempt to charge a premium because they know it is a car wreck case or a trucking crash and so they bill higher. When you hire the Parker Law Firm, we get involved immediately and start working with these medical care providers so that you are not getting gouged. We work on your claim in every conceivable way and allow you to concentrate on getting better. At Parker Law Firm, People truly do Matter.

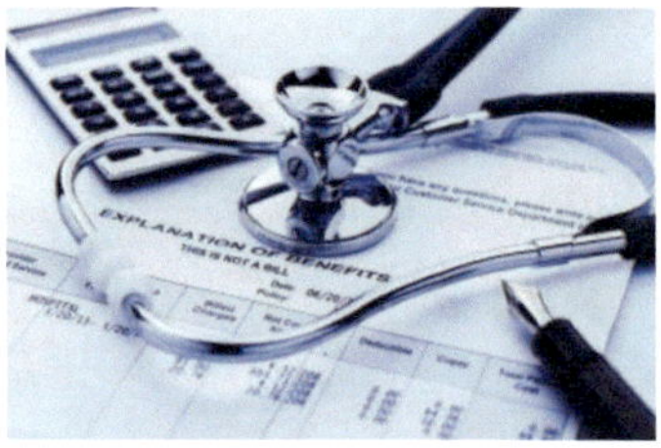

And, our fee will NEVER exceed your recovery.

What Are The Most Common Types Of Accidents Seen In Texas?

The types of accidents most commonly seen involve distracted drivers. One can hardly drive down the road without seeing somebody on their telephone or looking at a text on their smartphone. Many of the car wreck cases handled by Parker Law Firm involve distracted driving. Studies have repeatedly shown that distracted driving is just as dangerous–if not more so–than driving drunk. Distracted driving encompasses many things including eating, drinking, tuning the radio, or trying to use your smartphone. The vast number of smartphones being used has created a huge problem with driving and texting.

The Law In Texas Right Now On Cellphone Drivers

Different communities and localities have different laws in place. Some have laws that will prevent you from talking on a cellphone that is not hands free, while other communities prohibit the use completely while driving. Texas as a state, does not currently have any uniform law in place other than you cannot talk on a cell phone in a school zone.

What Is A No-Fault State?

Texas is NOT a No-Fault state. No-Fault means that rather than relying on the person who hits you for their insurance coverage, you rely on your own coverage! Texas is known as a third-party state which means that the person who causes the accident is the one primarily liable for any injuries caused by the crash. They are held accountable.

In Texas, there is form of No-Fault Insurance which is commonly referred to as Personal Injury Protection (PIP) or Medical Payment Coverage (Med Pay). You can buy that coverage yourself and it will help with some of the deductibles and out of pocket co-pays that you experience immediately. Typically, you will see PIP offered in a range of $2,500 to $10,000. It is a very good insurance to buy because it will help you with your out of pocket expenses long before any recovery from the third party insurance. Since Texas is NOT a No-Fault state, attorneys look to the at fault party to compensate you for your full losses.

What Is The Time Limit For Bringing A Personal Injury Lawsuit In Texas?

You have two years from the date of the crash in which you have to bring suit if necessary. Unfortunately, a lot of people think that they do not need to get a lawyer right away because they have two years in order to file a lawsuit, which is not true at all.

Many times, it is necessary to get a lawyer involved immediately so that evidence can be preserved, witness statements can be taken, cell phone records obtained and to work out medical liens and subrogation issues. If you wait until the last minute, other problems can arise, such as the defendant driver or the person who caused the crash may have moved and cannot be located. In case you cannot find them, then you are not going to be able to sue them. Even if you file suit before the expiration of the two year limitations period, the law requires service on the defendant immediately which can lead to the suit being dismissed if not served extremely quickly.

So the simple answer is, it is two years from the day of the crash, but if you have been seriously injured in an automobile crash, you need to seek counsel immediately. Delays only work to hurt your case.

What Is Classified As A Hit-And-Run Accident In The State Of Texas?

Any time someone makes physical contact with their car against your car and then flees the scene that is a hit and run.

Misunderstandings About Hit-And-Run Accidents

The biggest misconception is that they can somehow figure out who hit you. Unless you have witnesses or unless someone comes forward, the chances of finding out who actually hit you are pretty slim. That is all the more reason to get an attorney involved immediately.

Also, even if you have UI/UIM coverage, you have to be sure that you can prove that the damage to your car was as a result of a hit and run as opposed to just maybe you running into something and claiming it was a hit and run. Remember, the insurance company always wants to blame you. Many people do not understand that even though it was a hit and run, there may not be much that can be done about it or that they are going to have to fight their own insurance company to even get compensated.

Role Of An Attorney In These Cases

If you truly cannot locate the person who hit you, then you may need an attorney to just focus on the UI/UIM coverage that you have hopefully purchased. Unfortunately, a lot of times people try to save money and do not purchase UI/UIM insurance, in which case there is not much that can be done.

Who Can Be Held Responsible In A Hit-And-Run Case If You Cannot Find The Person Who Hit You?

If you cannot find the person who hit you and ran, then nobody is going to be held responsible. You can hope to recover under your UI/UIM coverage if you purchased it. If you have not, then there is probably nothing that can be done. Even if you have purchased UI/UIM coverage, you still might have a fight on your hands with your own insurance company when they dispute the fact that someone else actually hit your car.

Does Uninsured/Underinsured Motorist Coverage Cover Hit-And-Run Accidents?

It does as long as there was physical contact between the automobiles. Often times, people might call it a hit and run where a pickup truck is driving in front of them and a piece of the furniture falls out into the road right into their lane of travel and strikes the fallen furniture. The truck driver continues to drive on without even realizing what just happened. They might not even know until they get to their location that they have lost part of their furniture. In that situation, the UI/UIM insurance will not cover because there was no physical contact between the automobiles. Something falling out of a truck which is not part of the vehicle does not count for purposes of UI/UIM coverage.

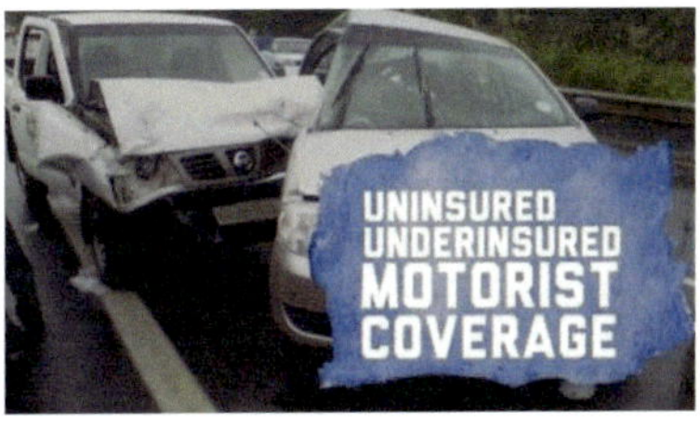

What Can You Do If There Is No Evidence Or Witness To The Accident?

If there are no witnesses or other evidence then only thing that can be done is to find whether there is a traffic or security camera that might have caught the accident. If there are no witnesses and you cannot identify the vehicle that hit you, then there is not much you can do. That is why you need to have your own UI/UIM insurance to make sure you are covered.

Misconceptions About Auto Accidents

Probably the biggest misconception that most people have is that all of their medical bills and all their economic damages are going to be paid by the at-fault driver. Insurance companies are in the business of making money – not spending it. They will fight even the rear end collision cases. However, more importantly, most people have very little insurance. If you are seriously injured in an automobile crash, often times there is not enough insurance coverage. This is especially so if there are more than 2 people injured.

The second biggest misconception is that the insurance company for the negligent driver will pay for your medical bills as they are incurred. Many times people will go to the hospital or see their doctors, and not want to use their own health insurance to pay for their bills thinking that the automobile insurance carrier will pay these bills. They will not do that. They will only make one payment and once that payment is made they will not make any other payments. Therefore, it is always best to have your doctors bill your health insurance company directly for the medical care they provide. Only once you have completely quit treating will your claim be ready for settlement.

Another big misconception is that you do not have to pay back the health insurance company that paid the medical bills. You MUST almost always have to pay back the health insurance company that paid for your medical bills from any settlement money that you receive. Subrogation issues and hospital liens can present very complicated scenarios in which medical providers and health insurance companies are entitled to part of your settlement money. Half of the battle is trying to defeat those subrogation and lien interests -- or at least minimize them. Most people do not understand all the intricacies that come into play once they receive a settlement from the insurance company.

If you are physically able, you want to get pictures of the scene. Pictures of the intersection, pictures of the cars involved, even a picture of the person who hit you. You want to trade information; you want to get all their insurance information. Take a picture of their insurance card. Then write down the information as well in case the picture does not turn out well, but often times the picture will give you information that you might forget later on.

The next thing of course, if you are injured, is to seek immediate medical attention. Many times, people involved in a car crash do not think that they are injured only to wake up the next morning and realize that something is terribly wrong with them. Seeking medical care as soon as possible is critical.

If you are taken away from the scene in an ambulance or seek medical attention immediately and are not able to take any pictures and get the insurance information, then be sure to contact, or have your family contact, an attorney immediately. The attorney can get involved and try to get the necessary information to pursue the at-fault party and protect your rights.

These are the immediate steps that need to be taken. You should not delay in interviewing and hiring an attorney. In the event you are seriously injured it is even more important that you hire a competent, board certified personal injury attorney to assist you as soon as possible.

Questions People Involved In Auto Accidents Ask

What Should You Do In Terms Of Insurance Companies If You Are Involved In An Auto Accident? Do You Have To Notify Your Own Or Other Party's Insurance?

First and foremost, if you or a loved one has been seriously injured due to the negligence of someone else, it is always best that you hire an attorney board certified in personal injury trial law as soon as possible. Contacting the other person's insurance first is always recommended. Contacting your own insurance company may result in an increase in your rates. However, depending on the circumstances your insurance company may eventually have to be contacted for any number of reasons. Therefore, you always want to see first and foremost about filing a claim against the person who caused the accident and depending on the types and amounts of coverages available, your insurance company may have to get involved.

Often times, you will need to call your insurance company to collect the PIP insurance or the Med Payment insurance which you purchased to help you with your out of pocket expenses. Those claims do not count as a mark against you and your insurance. Likewise, a claim against your own company may be necessary if the other party does not have enough insurance or is totally uninsured.

What Should Someone Do If Other Party's Insurance Company Contacts Them?

Never ever give a statement to the insurance company unless you are represented by an attorney and they are present to help you. Parker Law Firm strongly advises against giving any statements unless and until you are fully ready. One of the things you do not want to do is give a statement when you are hurt, you are still injured or you might be on medication. There may be things that you leave out or forget.

The number one thing to remember is that when you are talking to the other person's insurance company, they are not your friend. They are trying to get information that will assist them in either denying your claim outright or minimizing the amount they are going to have to pay on the claim based on things you may have inadvertently and very innocently said and that will be taken out of context.

If You Feel Fine Initially But Start Having Severe Pain Days Later That Requires Medical Treatment, Do You Still Have A Case?

You do, but the longer time goes by that you do not seek medical treatment, the more suspect the insurance companies become of your claim of injury. Moreover, jury's also become more suspect. That is why it is so important to be sure to go and get checked out by a medical professional as soon as possible if you are hurt. Often times as a result of the adrenaline from a crash, you will not realize that you have been hurt or something will not be readily apparent to you until the next day or the day after. That is when you want to be sure to go and get checked out.

Many people feel like they are okay and that they will get better in a few days and often times that is the case. However, you should still go and get checked out to be sure that there are no underlying problems. Any delay will not only affect your physical recovery and your wellbeing, but the delay certainly has the potential of diminishing your ability to get a full recovery.

Things To Take Care Of In An Auto Accident Case

Doctor's Advice

Following medical advice is extremely important. You need to follow the doctor's instructions. If they think you need physical therapy, you need to go to physical therapy. They are the doctors, they are the health professionals and if they ask you to do something and you do not do it, then the natural response is that "you must not be hurt very bad if you are not going to follow the doctor's advice."

Often times, the practicalities of daily living might prevent someone from being able to go to the doctor. Many times the injured are the sole bread winners of the family and they may be working through the pain because they cannot afford to take off work. Even if that is the case, you really need to find the opportunity and time at night, or on the weekends to seek treatment. Skipping your medical appointments will only jeopardize your case. If the doctor orders medical treatment you need to try your very best to follow through with it.

Often times, when you do not go to an appointment or you miss appointments, the insurance companies and defense attorneys consider that a gap in treatment or a gap in care and they use that to demonstrate that you are really not seriously injured. That is because if you really are hurt, you would want to go see a doctor. Remember, the insurance companies will use anything and everything against you to minimize your claim.

Evidence And Witnesses

Evidence is extremely important in cases where there is a he-said she-said type situation, which is often the case. Even in rear end collisions, we often hear the person who hit you claiming that you just jammed on your breaks suddenly and they could not avoid hitting you. If there are witnesses to an inter-section collision, you want to seek their information and what they can tell you about who had the green light versus the red light? All of those factors are extremely important.

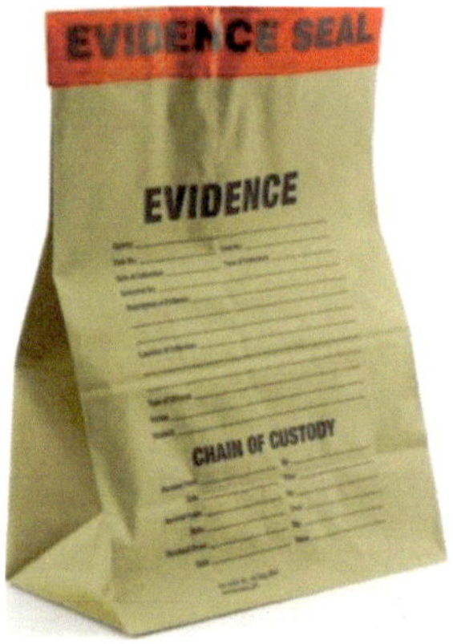

If there are witnesses that can testify about the at-fault party's reckless driving, then the likelihood of a jury or even the adjustor believing your version of events is greatly enhanced. Therefore, it is very important to get witnesses and gather any evidence that there might be including cellphone information and data if available.

Also, the number one reason for contacting an attorney early in the process is so that witness statements and evidence can be gathered. Remember, the insurance company is not there to help you. They are there to protect their insured and protect their profits. If they think they can avoid the liability of a claim, they will do it.

What Are The Minimum Insurance Requirements In Texas?

The minimum insurance requirements in Texas are $30,000 per person; $60,000 per incident. That means that each person driving on the road is supposed to have an insurance policy that will pay someone whom they injure up to $30,000. If there are two or more people in the car the insurance will pay up to $60,000 divided between all the occupants of the vehicle. That is not a lot of money in

the scheme of things. Especially if you are seriously injured, and spend much time in the hospital. One of the most beneficial types of insurance that you can have is UI/UIM or Under Insured/Uninsured Motorist Coverage. That is insurance that you buy for yourself and your family that will help pay the bills in the event that the person who hits you does not have enough insurance or they are completely uninsured.

What Rights To Compensation Do You Have If You Have Been In An Accident With An Underinsured Or Uninsured Motorist?

Your rights to compensation are going to be the same no matter what. The real question will be whether there are funds available to pay adequate compensation. That is why it is so important to have UI/UIM coverage that you purchase for yourself. Unfortunately, in Texas, the minimum insurance limits are $30,000. Most drivers who have insurance at all will only have $30,000. Therefore, if you are seriously injured, the availability of UI/UIM coverage becomes extremely important. It is amazing how many people are on the roads that have either minimum limits or no insurance whatsoever.

If you are seriously injured in an automobile accident, and you do not have UI/UIM motorist coverage, and the at-fault party has no insurance or even minimum limits, then compensation for injuries and losses is going to be very limited. That is why it is imperative to protect yourself against the negligence of other people. UI/UIM motorist coverage is some of the cheapest insurance that you can buy. While it may not seem cheap, it is cheaper than most insurance coverages and it is something that you really need to have in the event that you or a loved one is seriously injured in a car crash.

What Should You Do If The Driver Who Hit You Does Not Have Insurance Or Is Underinsured?

The thing that you do to protect yourself is to buy UI/UIM coverage before you ever need it. You are going to have to still establish the liability of the person who hit you and then turn around and make the claim against your own insurance company for UI/UIM coverage to apply. It is not an easy process and most insurance companies will fight their own insured by trying to minimize the claim. They nearly always assert that you were not really hurt, it was a preexisting injury or you are a malingerer. Your own insurance company will often times fight that the other party was not even liable for the accident and therefore UI/UIM does not apply.

It is a very complicated process and that is another reason why you absolutely need to hire a board certified personal injury lawyer in order to help you navigate these treacherous waters.

What If Someone Has The Urge To Go After An Uninsured Driver?

Pursuing a person that has no insurance is usually futile. It is going to depend entirely on what kind of assets the negligent party has. In Texas, many of your assets are exempt, making you judgment proof, which means that there is nothing to get. It is like the old saying, "you cannot get blood out of a turnip."

For example, your home in Texas is protected as your homestead; it cannot be subjected to pay a judgment. Your wages cannot be garnished. Your retirement account cannot be garnished. Your education fund for your children cannot be garnished. You cannot go after their car. If you can find a large bank account or an RV or airplane that is not otherwise exempt or heavily mortgaged you might be able to go after that, but only after you get a judgment and by that time most people are going to have either sold or hidden the asset.

Therefore, it is very difficult to sue someone who has no money and who has no assets. Unfortunately, the realities of the world are that most people work from pay check to pay check and are struggling to make ends meet on a weekly basis. If you are hurt or injured by someone who is just a hard working person trying to make ends meet, there are not going to be any assets to go after to fully compensate you. That is why it is so vitally important to have your own UI/UIM coverage.

Misunderstandings People Have About Uninsured Or Underinsured Drivers

A lot of people think that people that do not have insurance could go to jail. In reality, you cannot put someone in jail for not having insurance. They can and often times do lose their driver's license, but that is about the extent of it. At the risk of sounding like a broken record, this is again the number one reason you need to buy as much UI/UIM coverage that you can possibly afford – in order to protect yourself against those that are not responsible. The truth of the matter is that if you are involved in a serious car crash, your own UI/UIM may be the only insurance available to compensate you for your injuries.

Another misconception is the belief that by being required to have a minimum amount of auto insurance, that will be enough to fully compensate you if you are seriously injured by the negligence of another. It is often times not anywhere near enough. The only way that the injuries are going to be fully compensated is if they have protected themselves by buying UI/UIM coverage.

What Generally Is The Outcome In Underinsured, Uninsured Auto Accident Cases?

It depends. The real question becomes how much insurance is there, if any, and whether or not you have UI/UIM coverage. If there is no insurance coverage by the negligent party and you do not have UI/UIM coverage, then there is not much that can be done. Notwithstanding, Parker Law Firm has routinely sued uninsured or under-insured people with the desire of being able to get them to confirm in writing or under oath that they have no assets. Sometimes the fear of a lawsuit prompts them to find hidden money. Imagine that!

On the other hand, there are way too many occasions when the negligent person who hit them does not have any assets that a judgment could attach to. In those circumstances, there is little an attorney can do for them other than obtain minimum policy limits and go on from there.

However, in those circumstances where there is no or very little insurance, the attorneys at Parker Law Firm work very hard in negotiating with the medical providers who claim that they are owed money to significantly reduce if not waive their medical expenses, allowing our clients to at least recover something for their injuries.

WHY WOULD YOU NEED AN ATTORNEY TO HANDLE YOUR AUTO ACCIDENT CASE?

Most people involved in a car crash that was not their fault almost always need an attorney to obtain a fair settlement if they are seriously hurt. Their insurance carrier will not handle it for them. They will handle your property damage, assuming that you bought collision coverage. They will go ahead and take care of your car and if they believe that the other party is responsible, they will go ahead and take care of getting reimbursements for the property damage from the at-fault party's insurance company.

However, if you have been seriously injured, your insurance company is not going to pay you for your injuries unless the other side is liable; they pay their policy limits; and you have UI/UIM coverage. And then they are going to fight you on it. Your insurance company is just like the other person's insurance company when it comes to personal injury cases. They do not want to pay them. They want to make certain that they pay as little as possible on the claim. Therefore, you should hire an attorney board certified in personal injury trial law in order to make certain that all of the insurance companies involved pay in the way they are supposed to.

Can Someone Handle The Case On Their Own?

The answer to that question is sure, you can do that. You can even try and fly an airplane on your own, but do you really want to do something that you do not know how to do. How successful do you think that you would really be?

You have to keep in mind that processing these claims is not easy. It is a complicated intricate system that you are unfamiliar with unless you are in the industry, unless you are a lawyer, or unless you are an insurance adjuster. Moreover, the people that you will be dealing with are professionals. They know what they are doing. They handle these claims every day.

More importantly, many people do not understand that even if the insurance company is willing to write you a check tomorrow for the medical bills, you must still address the subrogation interests or hospital liens that need to be satisfied. And if you do not take care of those, you may find yourself being a defendant; being sued by your health care insurance company or the hospital seeking the amount of money that you just recovered to pay them back.

That is another reason why it is so important to get an attorney involved early in the process. Half the time, attorneys spend more time negotiating the subrogation and lien interests than they do actually getting the money. It is one thing to get the money and it is another thing to keep the money and you need legal help to do both. That is why it is so important to at least consult with a board certified personal injury attorney if you have been involved in a significant crash or other injury causing event that was not your fault.

Difference Between A Wrongful Death And A Survival Action Lawsuit

A wrongful death claim is based on the death of an individual and the claim is brought by either the spouse, the parents and/or the children of the deceased. Whereas a survival action is a claim that the deceased could have brought but for their death, and that claim is brought typically by the estate of the deceased.

Who Is Legally Entitled To Bringing A Wrongful Death Or Survival Action Lawsuit?

In Texas, a wrongful death statute provides that the parents, the children, or the spouse of the deceased can bring the action. Sisters, brothers, cousins, stepparents, and other relatives are not permitted under the statute to pursue a wrongful death claim. Under a survival action, it is typically the estate of the deceased who brings the action. If an estate has not been formally opened on behalf of the deceased, then often times, a personal representative of the deceased will bring that action. However, for legal reasons, an estate typically has to be opened at some point so that the claim can proceed.

Can A Family Be Involved In Both Of These Lawsuits At The Same Time?

Yes. Typically, both causes of action are brought by the family in the event of a death of a loved one. Sometimes, there are split families, due to divorce, estrangement or any number of other reasons. So many times the claims will be brought by two different factions of the family. One may be on behalf of the estate; the other may be brought by the parents, spouse or children of the deceased as wrongful death beneficiaries.

What Are The Common Types Of Injuries Or Accidents That Result In These Claims?

They are going to be very catastrophic and traumatic type injuries that cause the death of someone. All too often, motor vehicle accidents, trucking accidents, or work related injuries result in the death of a loved one; sometimes those types of accidents will result in the severe injury of a loved one and they may not succumb to their injuries for days, weeks, months or even years after the initial injury. Regardless, these claims are the result of very traumatic and catastrophic events that cause significant injuries that lead to death.

What Damages Are Family Members Entitled To In A Wrongful Death Lawsuit?

In wrongful death cases, the damages are in essence the loss of the love, the companionship, the society, the friendship that the survivor suffers as a result of their loved one being killed. The damages are based on the specific relationship between the loved one and the deceased. Obviously the damages can vary wildly depending on the nature, extent and duration of the relationship. The jury will be asked to consider such things as whether the parties were close or had day to day contact versus being somewhat estranged or had grown apart. Every relationship is different and it is the relationship between the loved one and the deceased that is evaluated in order to determine damages.

What Damages Is Someone Entitled To In A Survival Action Lawsuit?

Under a survival cause of action, the damages are for the harm suffered by the deceased before they passed away. For instance, how long did the deceased survive before succumbing to their injuries? Was there significant pain or discomfort involved? Was the deceased conscious and if so for how long? The survival action seeks to have the deceased's estate compensated for the pain, the suffering, the medical bills, and the impairment that they experienced during that period of time from the onset of the injury until the time of death.

Factors That Determine Viability Of A Wrongful Death Lawsuit

The typical factors considered include those considered in other personal injury cases. However, in a wrongful death matter the damages are based on the relationship of the loved one and the deceased as opposed to what the deceased endured from the tragic event. Under the common law, the courts did not recognize a wrongful death case. In other words, if the negligent party caused the death of someone, they could not be held liable to the family and that is why the wrongful death statute was created. Likewise, under common law, if you injured someone and they ultimately died, then the cause of action died with them. It was often said that it was cheaper to kill than to maim. That obviously was highly inappropriate and unacceptable and thus the legislature enacted a statute to specifically provide for these instances.

Challenges That Families Face In Wrongful Death Or Survival Action Lawsuits

The biggest challenges that families encounter as a result of the loss of the loved one are primarily emotional ones, but there are financial aspects as well. The deceased may have been the breadwinner, they may have been the one that was going to fund college, retirement for a spouse, and day to

day expenses. Because emotions are high, there can be significant discord among the family members making the decision of whether to pursue a claim problematic in and of itself. All of those are significant issues that arise in any kind of death case.

What Happens If One Family Member Is Against Filing The Lawsuit And The Rest Want To File?

If one or some of the wrongful death beneficiaries do not want to file the suit, the other wrongful death beneficiaries still can. This can still cause some problems down the line when it is time to settle the claim. The issue surrounds the fact that while there can be numerous wrongful death beneficiaries there can only be one wrongful death claim. In other words, there cannot be three or four different claims filed in different courts; they all have to be the same court under the same proceeding as opposed to different proceedings in different courts.

If there is someone who just does not want to be a part of it, that person can acknowledge their waiver of the claim and agree to give a release and not pursue the claim. Ultimately, if not all of the wrongful death beneficiaries want to pursue the claim, you must have them sign a waiver or they need to get a lawyer involved somehow, because at the end of the day, the defendants are not going to settle with part of the family and not all of the family that is entitled to be a wrongful death beneficiary.

How Are The Damages Divided Among Multiple Beneficiaries In A Wrongful Death Lawsuit?

In a wrongful death case, the case is going to be resolved either through settlement or through a jury trial. If the case goes to a jury, the jury is going to be asked to award damages based on each wrongful death beneficiary's relationship. The jury is going to allocate damages accordingly. The son may get one amount, a daughter a different amount. That is entirely based on the prerogative of the jury, and based on the relationship that each beneficiary had with the deceased.

If it settles on the other hand, then the wrongful death beneficiaries need to decide between themselves how it is going to be allocated. If they cannot agree, they must get separate lawyers to fight over how it is going to be allocated. That is part of the conflict that sometimes arises amongst the beneficiaries. If they cannot agree among themselves in the case of a settlement, then they are all going to need separate counsels.

With a survival claim, the damages are apportioned based on what the probate code or the will provides. There is a very elaborate scheme under the probate code that allows for distribution of assets of the estate based on whether or not they have a surviving spouse, based on whether or not they have surviving children, and based on whether or not their parents still survive them.

That is all statutorily pre-determined under the statute; or if they have a will, it will stand as the will provides.

How Are Damages Determined In These Lawsuits?

The damages in a wrongful death case base on the loss of the relationship that the loved one and the deceased shared. The claim of a wife, who is in a loving relationship with her husband, will have a claim significantly different than the parents who are older and may not have had as much contact with the deceased. Minor children may have a claim drastically different than adult children who have already moved away. While all of those relationships are significant, they will have different and varying degrees of interaction between each other.

Under a survival cause of action, the damages are going to be determined the same as if the person had never died. Medical bills, pain, suffering, impairment and mental anguish that the person endured prior to their death and the loss of earning capacity that the person suffered as a result of their injury will all be considered.

It is very much like a personal injury case not involving death in that sense. All of the damages available under a typical personal injury case are generally available. It is just the fact that the estate is bringing that cause of action instead of the injured person.

Misconceptions About Wrongful Death And Survival Action Lawsuits

The biggest misconception involves who is actually allowed to pursue the actual lawsuit. Imagine that there are twins and one of them is injured in a catastrophic accident and dies. Many times, the surviving twin will suffer a huge emotional loss. Unfortunately, the law does not allow that twin or any sibling, for that matter, to have a cause of action for wrongful death. Most people believe that if you have any kind of a family relationship, you should be able to file a wrongful death case. The wrongful death statute only allows the parents, the spouse and the children to bring the wrongful death claim; not siblings, not aunts or uncles nor step-parents. There are countless examples of extended and blended families where the law acts as an injustice. You can imagine the situation where maybe parents have predeceased the child and a child is raised by the aunt and uncle and then the child suffers some horrific accident, passes away and the aunt and uncle are barred from bringing any kind of wrongful death claim.

There are similar issues in pursuing a survival claim. Often times, there may have been divorced parents, and their child is killed in an automobile accident or trucking accident and both parents want to bring a survival cause of action. They cannot both bring it; it belongs to the estate. And so if they cannot agree and there has been no independent executor appointed, you have an issue of who has the legal right to bring that cause of action on behalf of the estate for the survival action. There is often times confusion and misconceptions with clients not having a full appreciation and understanding of who is entitled to file these claims.

If Several People Are Entitled To Bringing A Lawsuit, Does Each Person Have To Hire Separate Counsel?

Sometimes yes and sometimes no. Most of the time, in most of these kinds of cases, as long as the loved ones can agree, one attorney can probably file the entire suit. It needs to be understood that there is an inherent conflict that can arise by one attorney handling it. For instance, if one attorney represents all of the wrongful death beneficiaries, then they must agree on how any settlement will be divided. If a dispute between the beneficiaries arises the attorney cannot take the side of one of the beneficiaries over the other. In this situation, it may be necessary for each wrongful death beneficiary to retain separate counsel.

If the family can deal with the issue of how the proceeds from a wrongful death claim will be divided among them, then they can waive that conflict. If the family members are antagonistic against one another, then they are going to have to have separate attorneys for the wrongful death claim. Likewise, in a statutory survival action, if the family members cannot agree on who should bring the survival cause of action assuming no estate's been opened or there is no will, then there could be a conflict between the heirs and if they cannot agree on who should control the estate then they would need separate attorneys.

What Is The General Timeline For Resolution Of These Lawsuits?

Typically, you can expect that it will be two years from the date of the filing of the lawsuit to its completion. Most cases will resolve short of that timeframe depending on numerous factors. It can depend on how blatant was the negligence of the defendant, how much insurance coverage is available, how hard are the defendants going to contest liability, and what venue or forum is the case filed are but a few of the factors that can play a role in how long a case may last. Unfortunately, in Texas, the minimum amount of insurance that each driver has to have is $30,000. If a driver causes the death of someone else due to an accident in their car and it is their fault, those claims are typically going to resolve rather quickly.

On the other hand, if a loved one is killed by a trucking company who has lots of insurance and lots of assets, then those cases are going to drag out because the insurance company and the trucking company are going to contest the amount of damages.

The relationship between the deceased and the survivor are going to be very much an issue and so that is going to play a large role in delaying the process. Then again, the larger the company and the more assets at stake, the harder they are going to fight on liability. The timeline can be anywhere from a few months to as much as two years. It is really going to depend on a number of different factors.

Importance Of Retaining An Experienced Attorney For A Wrongful Death Or Survival Action Lawsuit

Unfortunately, insurance companies never automatically pay out. They always or almost always contest the claim in some form or fashion and therefore, you need to hire an attorney to help you through that process and force them to pay the claim as they should. It becomes even more complicated when they want to pay the claim, and you may have competing interests. Many families are blended and have different personalities involved and there may be some disagreements over what each family member should receive for their loss, especially if there is a survival cause of action. In a survival claim there is going to be some medical bills. Those medical providers need to be paid.

If there was any health insurance that was used to treat the deceased's injuries before their death, the insurance carriers are going to want to be reimbursed. In many situations, you have a scenario where the money is being tendered, but there are so many different interests trying to get a portion of that money that a lawyer needs to be involved just to help navigate those waters. As the case on any significant injury, and especially when death is involved, the more the defendant or the negligent party has in the way of assets or insurance the more they are going to fight, the more they are going to try to minimize the claim, and the more they are going to try and delay payment in the hopes of wearing down the loved ones.

Additionally, it is essential to appreciate and understand that the insurance company's representatives and lawyers do this for a living. They do it every day as their job. They get paid by dragging matters out and not paying the claims or at least trying to minimize it to the greatest extent possible.

Someone who has experienced the loss of a loved one is going through significant emotional trauma themselves, not only are they not trained to handle these types of claims, it is outside of their expertise; it is not what they typically do on a day to day basis. The beneficiaries are laboring under the emotional loss of a loved one which makes the whole process even that much more difficult and nerve-wracking. These are very complicated cases from start to finish and it is imperative to hire a competent, experienced and board certified attorney at the earliest possible moment to pursue the claims.

DISCLAIMER

This publication is intended to be informational only. No legal advice is being given and no attorney-client relationship is intended to be created by reading this material. If you are facing legal issues, whether criminal or civil, seek professional legal counsel to get your questions answered.

Parker Law Firm
2317 Plaza Parkway, Suite 100
Bedford, TX 76021
(817) 503-9200
www.parkerlawfirm.com
brad@parkerlawfirm.com

Made in the USA
Monee, IL
05 November 2026

67386575R00040